D1302488

THE HERO EFFECT

Being Your Best When It Matters The Most

KEVIN BROWN

In memory of
My mother, David, Denise, and Ted

Dedicated to
My dad, Lisa, Joshua, Kayleigh and Maddie

Thank you
To my closest friends. Your love and encouragement made this possible.
You know who you are and I love you.

TABLE OF CONTENTS

Introduction: The World Needs Heroes

The world needs heroes.

And by heroes I don't mean people running around wearing tights and a cape (unless you are into that).

What I mean is this: The world needs people who lead, love, and serve at a higher level. People who help us dream big dreams, achieve great things, and leave us better than they found us. People who exceed expectations and defy comparison. Those who make even the harshest critics stop in their tracks and admire the work.

The world needs heroes.

The brave ones who achieve the impossible in spite of the odds. Those who dare to act and bring forth that which was invisible to all but them.

The strong ones who shoulder the load when life gets hard and gives hope to the hopeless and breathes life into those who can't seem to catch their breath.

The brilliant ones who create, innovate, and make life easier—those who draw upon their unique genius to bring forth fruit that might otherwise find its way one day to the graveyard.

The world needs its heroes.
The problem solvers, the healers, the teachers, and preachers among us. The defenders and protectors of freedom.

Those who are willing to bring their best stuff to the present moment and pour it into the lives of others. To be their best when it matters the most. To inspire, motivate, and equip us for this journey we are all taking together. To clarify our mind, purify our heart, and edify our soul.

Indeed, the world needs heroes.
This book is about what happens when extraordinary people show up and choose not to be ordinary. After all, you weren't created for an ordinary life. Not for one minute.

CHAPTER 1

IT ALL STARTED WITH A QUESTION

I sat there staring at my yellow pad. It had one word scribbled on it—the word "hero." It was underlined and circled.

I was preparing a speech that I would deliver in three months. Two thousand people would pack a ballroom to hear this speech—a speech that I didn't have.

The idea was born out of a conversation with a friend. The group was a best-in-class organization—number one in their industry. Hard working, been-there-done-that kind of folks. The franchisees for this organization did the hard work of helping people put their lives back together in the wake of disasters big and small.

The word "hero" was a reference to the DNA of this group of people, a testament to how their customers felt about them. A quiet confidence permeated their attitudes and their actions. I wanted to honor the heroic efforts they put forth day in and day out, and I wanted them to know that they matter and that the work they do is important. I was committed to giving the speech.

But I was struggling.

I had given talks before but never anything like this. I had done the typical executive speeches. You know the kind: leadership, vision, communication, and customer service— the types of speeches we've all heard at some point in our lives.

This was different.

How was I going to talk about what it meant to be a hero at work and in life? What did I have to say about that?

Panic set in. I was officially freaking out.

CHAPTER 2

CAPTAIN FREAK-OUT

I don't know what you do when you freak out. But when I freak out, I go to my inner circle—the people who know, love, and support me unconditionally.

I went to my inner circle, and I asked (both of them) what I should do. I explained that I was freaking out about this hero speech and didn't even know where to begin.

One of the members of my inner circle is my wife, Lisa. For twenty-one years, I have had the privilege of being married to her. When I tell you that I married way over my head, that is a huge understatement. She is gorgeous on the outside and equally as beautiful on the inside. She is the most positive person I know, and I love her more than anything else on the planet. (And I do everything she tells me to do, because I am still afraid she might leave.)

She has a way of calming me down and getting me to focus on the task at hand. She knew I was in full-on freak-out mode and wanted to help. She sat down with me, took me by the hands, and said, "Honey, you are overthinking this like you always do. When you get on that stage just tell your story. Tell those people about your life." She paused and then added, "Everyone can learn from failure, poor decisions, and bad judgment."

She kissed me on the cheek and said, "Besides, honey, everybody feels better about their life once they've heard about yours."

I still love her. But she is no longer part of my inner circle.

I'm kidding of course. She is the *foundation* of my inner circle.

But I kept hearing her sweet voice in my ear, her words bouncing around in my head: "Just tell your story…"

I went back to her and said, "Help me understand. How does that help me talk about heroes?"

CHAPTER 3

THE FACES IN THE MIRROR

She said, "Let me explain it this way. When you look in the mirror, do you see yourself or all the people who helped you become you?"

"Do you see the people who helped you when you couldn't help yourself?"

"How about the people who picked you up when life knocked you down?"

"Do you see the people who loved you when you were unlovable (and believe me, there were lots of times)?"

She continued, "If you don't see those faces, then you are missing the picture completely. Hopefully, you understand, Mr. Brown, that you are not a self-made man. You are the sum total and the by-product of everyone who has ever shown up in your life. Think about all the people who have stopped by and poured a little bit of themselves into you— leaving you better than they found you. Some were there for a moment and some for a lifetime. If you want to talk about heroes, start there."

It reminded me of a story I heard about Muhammad Ali. He was on a plane that began experiencing turbulence. The flight attendant asked him to fasten his seat belt. Ali quipped, "Superman doesn't need a seatbelt."

The flight attendant fired right back saying, "Superman doesn't need an airplane either. Please fasten your seatbelt."

The truth is that no one gets there on his or her own. We all need help moving from where we are to someplace new. We need help getting to the next level. We need help becoming more of who we were born to be.

People flow in and out of our lives, some for a minute and some for a lifetime.

Some indirectly.

Some in your face.

Some by your side.

I raced back to my yellow pad, turned to a clean sheet, and wrote a question across the top of the page.

CHAPTER 4

What Does a Hero Look Like?

That question was, "What does a hero look like?" It loomed large on the fresh sheet of yellow paper. I sat and pondered that question, thinking through the lens of what Lisa had said. Closing my eyes, I thought about all the people who had helped me along the way.

I got up from my yellow pad and went and stood in front of the mirror and stared at myself for an uncomfortable amount of time. The minutes ticked by, and then my image began to fade. I started to see the faces of my heroes. I saw my parents. I saw teachers and preachers, friends and family. I saw coworkers and colleagues and even the faces of a few people I barely knew at all—but they had made a difference in my life.

With these images foremost in my mind, I went back to my yellow pad and the question that was begging for an answer.

What does a hero look like?

And I was still stuck. How do you define such a group of people? All of them different. All of them special. All of them having made their own unique contribution to my life. I wondered, "What was the common thread?"

How do you define the word "hero"?

I grabbed pad and pencil and set out to pose that question to everyone I knew and some that I didn't. I wanted to know how the world at large defines this idea of being a hero.

CHAPTER 5

THE GOLD STANDARD

The first thing I began to hear about was our military men and women—the defenders and protectors of freedom. The ones who go to work every day for a little bit of money and do so much for millions of people whom they will never meet. Faces they will never see. Names that they will never know.

We cannot have a conversation about heroes without honoring the men and women who keep us safe and keep us free. Those who allow us to live out our dreams in the greatest nation on planet earth. These brave men and women are the real deal when it comes to the business of being a hero. They are the gold standard in the hero world.

And far too often they are invisible.

I live in airports. I see these heroes among us, blending in, virtually unnoticed by the people they go to work for every single day. Tragic.

CHAPTER 6

You Can Never Go Wrong Doing the Right Thing

Chad is one of my best friends in the world. He is also married to a Lisa, which makes it very easy for us. We cannot mess it up: Lisa and Lisa.

Chad's Lisa is a sweetheart and a dear friend to us. She is also the most patriotic human being I have ever known in my life. If she sees men or women in uniform, she is going to hug them, love them, thank them, and buy them a meal if we are anywhere near food.

Whenever I am in town on a Friday night, the four of us go out for dinner. One Friday night we were sitting in a Cracker Barrel. (Because we're big spenders, and that's where we take our girls.)

We were sitting there talking and having a good time when through the door came a guy wearing fatigues. The three of us looked at each other and grinned. We'd seen this movie before and knew exactly what was about to happen.

Sure enough, the hostess seated the guy a couple of tables over from us, and before we could blink, Chad's Lisa was on the move. She made her way over to his table and sat down across from him. Freaked him out completely.

He started to push himself back from the table. Simultaneously Lisa reached across the table, grabbed his hands, and pulled him close. She said "Sir, I just want to thank you for your service to our country. I want to thank you for going to work every day to keep us safe and keep us free. Thank you for keeping my boys safe. I have two of them. Thank you for keeping my dogs safe. I have two of them—shelties. Thank you for keeping my husband safe. I have just one of those."

And it's always in that order: the boys, the dogs, then Chad.

This guy was stunned. He was wide-eyed and speechless.

But Lisa wasn't finished. She leaned in and said, "Sir, it would be my honor to buy your meal as a small token of appreciation for all that you do."

The guy had had all he could stand. He let go of her hands, leaned back, and said, "Aw, ma'am, I'm not in the military. I've just been out huntin'."

We cracked up. She was so embarrassed she turned three shades of red and came back to the table. So we did what any good group of friends would do: we made fun of her. I mean we wore it out—we did the voice and made the same gestures as the hunter did.

After twenty minutes or so, she'd had enough. Chad knew it was time to knock it off or the rest of his night was not going to be much fun. He said something to his Lisa that was absolutely profound and a relevant starting place for this conversation about heroes.

He looked at his bride and said, "Baby, you can never go wrong doing the right thing."

Powerful words. You can never go wrong doing the right thing. You can never go wrong treating someone with kindness and respect. Not because there is something in it for us—but by virtue of their status as a human being, they have already earned it.

You can never go wrong doing the right thing.

Yes, we bought a hunter's meal that night. So what? In fact, if you're ever in Nashville, throw on some huntin' clothes and head over to the Cracker Barrel. We'll see you there.

We live in a world that has strayed so far from the fundamentals of kindness and human decency that it is no wonder I hear from companies and organizations all over the country that need help with culture, relationship building, engagement, and customer loyalty.

We live in a society where people have become indifferent and blind to each other. We need to be rewarded to muster up some good old-fashioned kindness. Tuned in to that one station, WIIFM ("what's in it for me"?). What's in it for you is the opportunity to deliver what's in it for them. And when you do that, you automatically get what's in it for you and then some.

Everything it seems, at work and at home, is built on conditions. I will do this for you if you do this for me. We hold each other to the letter of the contract. Every encounter is a transaction or negotiation.

Heroes don't think that way.

CHAPTER 7

WHAT IS IT ABOUT THE GREAT ONES?

Armed with my one question and a yellow pad, I continued my quest for answers. I wanted to know the qualities and characteristics of a hero.

Why do we pull certain people out of the pile and place them on a pedestal? We single out the great ones, lift them up, and designate them as the gifted ones, as the anointed few with some special dispensation from God to be greater than all the rest.

As I kept asking the question, people would talk about all the "categories" of heroes in their world.

They talked about world changers like Nelson Mandela, Martin Luther King Jr., and Mother Teresa.

They spoke of first responders and caregivers, the doctors and nurses who nurture and heal us when we are broken.

I heard stories of teachers and tutors and the coach who made all the difference in a young life—the neighbor, the friend, the stranger who helped in a moment of need.

They were singing the praises of their favorite sports heroes: Michael Jordan, Peyton Manning, Tom Brady, and LeBron James. They would tell how the great ones can take an ordinary sport and make it look special—playing the same game as everyone else, but at a level that made it an art form unto itself.

They talked about the great brands they do business with and how they love to spend their money with companies that exceed their expectations and offer an experience they don't get anywhere else. We make choices using our money and time and attention every day and invest where we feel we get the best return. When we don't, we stop investing. Most of the time we don't even announce it. We just stop and move our dollars, time, and attention someplace else.

As I continued to ask the question, a pattern began to develop. I must have asked two hundred people the question, "What does a hero look like?" And almost every single time, I heard the same words:

Heroes are ordinary people who do extraordinary things.

At first, it sounded right. I thought that was absolutely the definition we have placed upon heroes in our society. Turn on the news, read the newspaper, and you will most certainly hear those words to describe a hero.

After hearing it over and over again, I began to wonder, "Is that really true?" Are heroes really just ordinary people doing extraordinary things, or have we been conditioned to think about heroes in a dangerous way? Have we, in fact, been convinced that somehow we were all born ordinary and are destined to spend our lives living as ordinary people with only the occasional burst of "extraordinary"?

CHAPTER 8

BORN EXTRAORDINARY

The day you were conceived a miracle occurred.

Science tells us that when you were dropped off at the pool, there were around a hundred million other kids dropped off that same day—one hundred million applicants for the job of being you. And only you got through.

You started working, paddling your way through the crowd. Out of the shallow end and into the wide-open ocean of pure possibility. Wearing your tiny cap and goggles, you started moving, and all of a sudden, you hit your stride. Like a little Michael Phelps swimming for gold, you crossed the finish line first. You made it through. You beat the odds. You became the miracle. And nine months later, you received your gold medal: the gift of an unblemished canvas on which to paint the story of your life.

Sounds pretty extraordinary to me.

Created in the image of perfection. A miracle at birth, endowed with the talents, gifts, and abilities that are as unique as your fingerprints. There's nothing ordinary about that in my book. Perhaps we've had it wrong the whole time. Maybe we've been conditioned to think about heroes in the wrong way, leaving us to believe that it's OK to be ordinary most of the time and only occasionally let our extraordinary selves shine through.

CHAPTER 9

ORDINARY IS A CHOICE

What I began to realize is that ordinary is a choice. Do you buy that? It's absolutely true.

Ordinary is a choice that keeps extraordinary people from their best lives. It suppresses greatness and fosters a false sense of averageness that manifests itself as a lifetime of mediocrity.

What began to stir in me was this idea that the great ones think just the opposite of everyone else. The reason we pull them out of the pile is that they *think* and *act* differently. They show up with their best stuff when it matters the most. They understand that they were born extraordinary, and they show up every day and choose not to be ordinary. They are willing to do the hard work of digging it out of the dirt, putting in the time, effort, and mental focus to bring forth their extraordinary gifts.

CHAPTER 10

BONSAI OR BAMBOO

When I think about the difference between ordinary and extraordinary, I think about the bonsai tree and the bamboo tree. Both are beautiful in their own right. But one spends its entire life as an unrealized potential, and the other stands boldly in its destiny.

The bonsai tree is an ancient art form and a great metaphor when it comes to superhuman living. The bonsai tree is intentionally created to be a miniature version of itself, carefully and meticulously pruned and stunted into a beautiful work of art that resembles all the splendor and glory that it could have been if it had been allowed to grow and reach its true potential.

The bamboo tree, on the other hand, is destined to reach for the heavens at its appointed time. Planted, protected, and cared for each and every day. Day after day its caregiver waters, nurtures, and provides what it needs to grow. Day after day. Month after month. Year after year.

And nothing happens.

For five years.

And then one day, encouraged by the radiant glow of the sun, a tiny bamboo shoot breaks through the soil and rockets toward the sky, growing a stunning ninety feet in only five weeks—an amazing accomplishment.

An overnight success that was five years in the making.

Unfortunately, far too many people go through life as a bonsai tree, a miniature version of all they could have been. Intentionally stunted by their own hand to be less than they were created to be.

Here is the amazing part: I have read that it takes between two and twenty years to create the perfect bonsai tree—years of painstaking and dedicated work in order to stay small.

The bamboo tree takes five years of diligent effort and care—every day doing the work while not seeing immediate results. But behind the scenes, all of that work has been making the bamboo tree strong, making it ready for the world. And when it finally breaks through, it takes off and reaches heights the bonsai tree will never know.

You see, most people do a little bit of work, and if they don't see results, they dig up that seed and go start all over again someplace else. They find another pile of dirt and attempt to put down roots, only to become frustrated too soon and give up. They are in a constant state of stop and start. They want instant gratification and are too impatient to do the hard work of realizing their true potential. Created to reach for the sky, instead they remain content to live in their own shadow. They quit right before they achieve the breakthrough.

The bottom line is that it takes just as much or more work to be a small, ordinary version of yourself as it does to be the giant, extraordinary version you were born to be.

Do yourself and the world a favor, and choose to be a bamboo tree.

CHAPTER 11

TRUSTING THE CAPE

The one person I wanted to talk to and ask what a hero looked like was the ten-year-old version of myself. Kids have a brilliant way of seeing themselves and the world. They are confident. They think they showed up with all the right stuff. They believe they are here to save the world, help people, and make a positive impact.

Adulthood has a way of squeezing that out of us (along with some other stuff). We get wrapped around the proverbial axle of life, and somewhere along the line, we are convinced that there's nothing special about us. We become content to get by, flying below the radar. We tell ourselves—and others—not to make waves, that we're living the dream, when all we're doing is simply trying to survive.

And yet the only people who have ever done anything significant were the people who flew above the radar, raised their hands when the game was on the line, and shouted "put me in, coach!" They made some waves. Getting by wasn't part of their vocabulary. "Live fully and thrive" is their philosophy.

When I was a kid, I wanted to be a superhero. I thought it was a job you could get.

An astronaut.
A cowboy.
Superhero.

I wanted to be Superman. I thought I had superpowers and could change the world and make a positive difference. I thought I had something extra and was destined for greatness. I even thought I could fly.

I used to tie a bath towel around my neck and run through the house jumping off furniture pretending to fly. It drove my mother crazy. (My wife doesn't like it either.)

One day I had my cape on, and it was working well. Flying with ease, I was running through the house jumping off furniture pretending to fly. First, the couch. I jumped and flew three feet. Then I climbed the kitchen cabinets next to the refrigerator. I took a deep breath and jumped. This time I flew five feet. I was feeling very confident, so I went outside and climbed the tree next to our garage and got onto the roof of the garage. I walked to the edge of the roof and stared at the driveway below. I had confidence and trusted the cape to do its job.

I took a deep breath, tugged on the cape, and with out-stretched arms, I jumped. And I flew—straight down. I landed in the driveway with a thud. My lip started to quiver, and I could feel tears welling up in my eyes. "Superman doesn't cry," I said quietly to myself while holding my knee. My mom heard the commotion and, in one superhuman leap from the house to the driveway, swooped in to rescue her baby boy. She picked me up, dusted me off, checked me for bruises, and kissed me on the forehead. Then she spanked me like I have never been spanked before in my life.

And from that moment on, Superman was grounded. And over time, that kid forgot that he could fly.

Have you forgotten how to fly?

When we were kids we looked at the world differently. We believed in something bigger than ourselves. We could close our eyes and escape to a place where not even the sky was the limit.

CHAPTER 12

DECORATE THE BOX

When we were kids, we lived for the day when someone in the neighborhood bought a washer or dryer.

Why? Because we wanted the box.

Why? Because to us, it wasn't a box.

Limited only by the boundaries of our imagination, that box represented anything we wanted it to be: a race car, an army fort, a spaceship. And if we got really lucky, someone would buy a new refrigerator. Cha-ching. We had won the lottery. Now we had a time machine.

When we were kids, we would decorate the box. And that box would transport us from where we were to someplace better. Someplace new. We could spend hours playing with that simple cardboard box.

And then we grew up.

Somewhere between imagination and limitation, we grow up. We begin "pruning" that kid out of our life—stunting our creativity and leaving us with the box we live and do business in. The box that we believe is so restrictive that we must do all of our thinking outside of it when in fact, we have all the capacity to decorate the box just like when we were kids.

When we get older, we are confined, conformed, and defined by the box we're in. And the box is really nothing more than the rules of the game. It's the policies, procedures, systems, and people that make up our world. Every arena of endeavor has its rules—a box where the players reside and the game is played. For some, it's a field or a court. For others an office or a cube. For some it's their home or the open road. Regardless of the box, the great ones show up every day, limited only by their imagination, and decorate the box, painting with broad brush strokes of talent and ability to create a masterpiece on the canvas of their life. They play the same game as everyone else, but when they show up to do what they do, it looks special. It looks unlike the game everyone else is playing, even though they are subject to the same rules as everyone else. They don't conform to the box. Instead they transform the box. They bend, shape, twist, and color the box in a way that makes it into something new. The box becomes their own personal playground of productivity and achievement. A canvas upon which to paint their next masterpiece.

CHAPTER 13

HERO REIMAGINED

If we buy into the idea that heroes are ordinary people doing extraordinary things, then by default we are giving ourselves permission to be average and mediocre most of the time. We have pushed integrity outside of ourselves, allowing us to simply be ordinary and only occasionally show up with our extraordinary self and do great things.

To commit to the choice of being ordinary, you must first convince yourself that you aren't anything special. You have to tell yourself over and over again that you have no purpose and no reason for being. The bottom line is that you must lie to yourself in order to sell yourself on the idea that you are ordinary in the first place.

I believe the people, organizations, and teams that we pull out of the pile and label as special think very differently than everyone else. I believe they are clear about the responsibility that comes with greatness. I believe they know beyond a shadow of a doubt that they were born with talents, gifts, and abilities that are unique to them and endowed with the potential to impact the world by using their passion to serve others well. I believe they show up every day with the intention of leaving it all on the field every single time they step up to the plate.

Let's reimagine this idea of being a hero. Instead of an ordinary person who does something extraordinary, let's redefine what it really means to be a hero.

A hero is an extraordinary person who chooses not to be ordinary!

You see, if we buy into the notion that everybody on the planet was born extraordinary, then we must concede that ordinary thinking is a learned behavior, a conditioned response based on the voices in our head. We've been convinced of our unworthiness. Our averageness shows up in the way we talk to ourselves and to others. We're "not good enough." "It will never work out." "It just wasn't meant to be." Or my favorite: "It is what it is." No, it's not. It is what you decide to make it, and it begins with understanding and believing that you were born extraordinary and have become ordinary by choice.

CHAPTER 14

THE FANTASTIC FOUR QUALITIES OF A HERO

Armed with my new paradigm, I began to look for the everyday heroes in my world, moving from the world stage to everyday life. I wanted to know what greatness looks like closer to home. Why do we gravitate to certain people and brands? Why are we drawn to them? How do they do what they do at a consistently high level and make us stop in our tracks and admire their work?

I soon realized that heroes do certain things better than everyone else. They show up with a different mind-set and focus. Specifically, I noticed four fantastic qualities that shine through every time the hero shows up.

Heroes *help* people—with no strings attached.

Heroes create an *exceptional* experience for the people they serve.

Heroes take *responsibility* for their attitude, their actions, and their results.

Heroes see life through the lens of *optimism*.

Now let's take a closer look at each one of these fantastic four qualities of a hero.

CHAPTER 15

Heroes Help People...with No Strings Attached

The first thing I began to notice about heroes in everyday life is that heroes help people. I realize there is nothing profound or revolutionary about that idea. I'm guessing that no one is scrambling to find a highlighter right now. Nobody ever jumps out of their seat in my keynote speeches and proclaims the profoundness of that little nugget of truth. In fact, you may have just rolled your eyes. And if you did, I get it. But stay with me for a minute.

Fundamentally we all get it. We all understand on some level that helping others is a key ingredient to success in life. We are taught that serving others is the pathway to making a difference and creating wealth. And yet even though we are taught this idea of servant hood, it has been my experience that most people actually don't get it. They understand it and perhaps even try to be helpful to the extent that it's worth *their* anticipated return on investment—if it is worth their time and attention to give a little something more for a greater something in return. In other words, there is a motive. There's quid pro quo. The truth is that we live in a conditional world. At work and at home. We are always bargaining, negotiating, and working an angle to get what we want.

Heroes don't do that.

What I discovered as I dug into this idea of helping others is that there is a part two that heroes execute instinctively. I began to notice that the heroes in everyday life—the ones we single out and recognize as different, the best of the best in their chosen arena—have reached another level in the area of serving others.

They have mastered the dot, dot, dot.

The dot, dot, dot?

Yes.

Heroes help people…with *no strings attached.*

No pretense. No conditions. No agreement. Here's where it rubs our humanness the wrong way. We're not wired to think in terms of "no strings attached." We live by the letter of the law, the contract rules. The transaction drives behavior. We think in terms of "I will do this for you if you do this for me."

Heroes don't think that way. Heroes understand that one of the greatest battles in this life is the the fight to suppress our humanness and embrace our humanity.

They approach their work and their life very differently. They bring a passion and a focus on the outcome for their customer that is different from almost everyone else in their space. They are not caught up in transacting business. They are deeply caught up, however, in transforming the moments and leaving the people they serve wanting more.

Heroes step up and deliver excellence every single time, and because of this, their fans evangelize their story to the rest of the world and drive new customers and more business to them again and again and again.

Are you a dot, dot, dot master?

Do you operate with a "no strings attached" mindset?

CHAPTER 16

THE ONLY PERSON IN THE ROOM

L et me paint a picture of what this looks like in everyday life. Her name is Rebekah and she is a dot, dot, dot master!

To set the stage I need to give you a little backstory.

I've had bad hair my whole life. People who have gone to college and hold advanced degrees in hair care have told me since I was a kid that my hair is difficult to cut. I am told it has a mind of its own and the texture falls somewhere between barbed wire and straw.

Having bad hair is one thing. Getting bad haircuts on top of that is another matter entirely. Trust me, it's not a good combination.

I was on a string of bad haircuts for more than a year. I tried salon after salon to no avail. I would come home after every haircut and complain to the most positive human being I know—my wife, Lisa.

After a year, she had had all she could handle. She decided to take matters into her own hands. She called her stylist and got a referral for someone to cut my hair. She called, made the appointment, and told me where to go (something I am very used to at this point in my life).

I showed up at the appointed time, and this place was packed. Flat-screen TVs on every wall. People in the waiting area. Hair flying everywhere. This place was busy.

As I stood there, a young lady in the back of the salon— a vivacious brunette with big blue eyes—noticed me. She flashed a giant smile and started walking toward me with an outstretched hand. She shook my hand and said, "My name is Rebekah. You must be Kevin." Surprised and caught off guard I replied, "I am. How did you know?"

She smiled and said, "Your wife described the haircut!"

I gave a half-hearted smile as I followed her to her station. I sat down in her chair, and immediately she began asking about my favorite subject: me.

"Your wife sounds sweet. Lisa, right?"

"How long have you been married? Any kids?"

"Where do you work? How long have you been there? Are you any good at it?"

She is asking me about my life. We are laughing and telling stories. You would have never guessed that we had met only five minutes earlier.

Rebekah drew me in with a smile. And then she mastered the dot, dot, dot.

She made me feel like I was the *only* person in the room.

Question: Do you make the people who mean the most to you feel like they are the only people in the room?

I love the way Rabbi Shmuley Boteach puts it:

"You are no hero if the people who mean the most to you think the least of you."

How do you make the people around you feel?
    What about the people who mean the most to you?
    Rebekah made me feel like her most important priority.

CHAPTER 17

MR. DELICIOUS

We were laughing and talking when Rebekah surprised me again. She began massaging my neck and shoulders.

I liked it. A lot.

As the tension slowly melted away, I found myself beginning to relax. Something that was far too uncommon in my fast-paced, stressed-out life. You see, heroes know instinctively that their job is to remove tension and solve problems. Every person on the planet is paid to solve problems. And to the degree you do it with excellence every time, that is what determines your happiness, wealth, and future opportunities. Heroes are great stewards of their relationships and resources. They maximize the potential of everything they have.

Rebekah is rubbing my shoulders. We are laughing and having the best time. It's like old home week. We talked like we were old friends.

This twentysomething never texted, tweeted, or posted anything even once. She didn't talk to the person to her right or to her left. She stayed focused on me the entire time. I know people twice her age who can't pull that off.

When she got done rubbing my shoulders, she took me over to a sink and washed my hair. And when she washed my hair, I forgot my name. You know what I am talking about when someone gives you a good head scratch and your eyes roll back and you melt.

She had me.

I liked it. A lot.

When she was finished washing my hair, she took me back over to her station and sat me in her chair. She put a cape over me, turned the chair away from the mirror, and started cutting my hair. She's working her magic and we're laughing. I am having the time of my life. Cut it all off. I don't care.

She gets done cutting and puts her scissors down. She steps back and gives me a good look up and down. She nods with self-approval and smiles. As she pulls the cape from around my neck, she slowly spins the chair around so I can face the mirror. As the chair is spinning around, she pulls the cape the rest of the way off and says:

"There you go, Mr. Delicious!"

I immediately felt flushed. What? Mr. Delicious! No one has ever called me Mr. Delicious. Say it again! Please say it again!

I was stunned. Overwhelmed. Feeling very good about myself.

The haircut just became secondary. She validated me. She noticed me. She made me feel special.

Let's review.

I am a middle-aged man. Nobody rubs my shoulders. Nobody washes my hair like that. I've tried to recreate it in the shower but I can't. (And I realize now that sounded better in my head.)

No one has *ever* called me Mr. Delicious!

I asked Rebekah if she calls all of her customers "Mr. Delicious."

She said, "Nope. Just you."

And I believe her.

Since then…

I have asked my staff to call me Mr. Delicious!

I have asked my wife to address me as Mr. Delicious!

When I speak to organizations, I always ask to be introduced as Mr. Delicious!

My requests have been denied 100 percent of the time.

I know what you are thinking. "C'mon, KB. Does giving someone a haircut really make them a hero?"

Yes. It does. If you understand that the role of a hero is to relieve stress and solve problems. My hair was a major source of frustration and stress. The experience of getting a haircut was a problem for me.

She relieved the stress and solved the problem. She made my life better.

Heroes always make life better.

Heroes are easy to do business with. They remove the complexities and make it simple. Heroes know that the easier it is to do business with them the harder it is for the competition to take their customers.

The market share you are fighting for is the emotional space between your customer's head and their heart. Logic tells. Emotion sells. If you make the emotional connection, your customer will fight to find the logic to support their decision to do business with you.

How is this relevant to you? It's relevant in a very profound way.

First, I am not suggesting that you call your customers and clients Mr. or Mrs. Delicious. Most likely that would be weird. Second, just to be clear, that name is already taken.

The point is that I will never ever go anywhere else for a haircut. I drive by at least twenty salons just to get to her, and I don't consider the others a viable option.

Excuse me? Did you say you drive by her competitors and don't even consider them an option? Correct. Many are closer and most are cheaper.

Doesn't matter. I'm a fan.

Isn't that what you want for your business? Isn't that what we want for our personal life with our friends and family? To be the only choice? The obvious choice? As Joe Calloway so brilliantly writes, to be that "category of one" company or person that defies competition.

Let's take a closer look at what Rebekah did to master the dot, dot, dot and serve with no strings attached.

CHAPTER 18

THE NON-NEGOTIABLES

Rebekah's operating philosophy starts with a non-negotiable mind-set. The playbook for how she has decided to run her life begins with a foundation of how she *chooses* to treat people, and for her it's non-negotiable. This is a common thread with heroes. They treat people right and own the moments that matter—and they know that every moment matters.

Rebekah moved beyond the conditions to create a connection with me. She has become family to us.

Ball game.

Most people and organizations today operate from a transactional perspective, meaning they are focused on the conditions of the contract. I will do this for you if you do this for me. They deal in the minimums required to get by.

Heroes think differently.

Heroes are not focused on conditions. Heroes are focused on connections. Heroes reach beyond what is required to achieve the remarkable. They begin with a philosophy of how they will treat others. Their foundation is rooted in the non-negotiables while everyone else is playing with the non-essentials.

What are the non-essentials?

Quite simply they are the excuses we make up for not serving others well. The non-essentials are all the busy work and fake priorities that we come up with that keep us from creating an above and beyond, wow-factor experience for those we serve. *Anything* that doesn't move the organization's top priorities and highest payoff activities forward is a non-essential.

It's anything that distracts and detracts you from bringing your best stuff to the present moment and pouring it into the lives of others. I don't need to give you a list. You know what keeps you from being your best. And the number one thing that keeps you from being your best is a *decision to be ordinary.* To show up and be like everyone else. To show up and do the minimum required to get by. To show up and do it like everyone else.

What are the non-negotiables?

This is where the rubber meets the road. Do you want to elevate your game? Decide what you stand for. Decide what will absolutely not be compromised in your life and in your work. Decide how people will define their experience with you. These things are the non-negotiables. This is your operational philosophy for life. This reaches beyond the borders of your professional life and into every area of endeavor.

The non-negotiable mind-set deals in absolutes. Those things that will absolutely not be compromised. Those things for which there is no bending and no flexing. Those things which you refuse to sacrifice at any price.

For Rebekah it is simple. When it comes to how she treats people she is resolute. She smiles and draws people in with her personality. She immediately takes a personal interest in them and demonstrates a caring attitude. She then goes about the business of delivering more than anyone expected. Exceeding expectations in every way.

Rebekah is a shining example of what it means to transcend the conditions of the relationship and create a connection that changes everything. Rebekah is not wrapped around the axle of transacting business. She is in fact in the business of transforming the encounter completely and, in the process, creates raving friends and fanatical followers who tell her story for her. That's how you build your personal and professional brand!

Remember—no one tells your story like an enthusiastic customer!

What story do people tell about their experience with you?

CHAPTER 19

VALIDATION

I was watching an interview with Oprah. She was retelling a portion of the commencement speech she had delivered at Harvard, and I was struck by her comments.

What she said summed up perfectly what I believe to be true about humankind and why some people draw you in like a magnet and others send you running in the opposite direction.

She was talking about all the people she had interviewed over her career on *The Oprah Winfrey Show*. She had interviewed some thirty-five thousand guests when she retired and moved into the next chapter of her life to start her *own* television network.

Here was the conversation:

Oprah was talking about the common thread shared by all the people she had interviewed. She said that everyone she had ever interviewed was seeking validation—from the rich and famous to everyday people.

It didn't matter whether it was President Bush, President Obama, or Beyoncé. When the cameras stopped rolling and the lights were turned off, they all leaned over and said, "Was that OK?"

They wanted to know if they had done well. They wanted to be validated. It didn't matter whether they were the best or worst in the world at what they did or the leaders of the free world.

They wanted to know if they had done a good job.

I love the way Oprah summed up this idea of validation. She attached three questions to this concept:

Do you see me?
Do you hear me?
Does what I say even matter to you at all?

I would suggest to you that all the people in your life, whether you know them well or you just met, are all asking the same three questions.

They are all craving for validation, longing to be recognized for their unique gifts. And when they don't get it, it's like cutting oxygen off to their identity. It leaves a hole in their heart that can only be filled by the someone willing to give them undeniable evidence that they matter.

What a powerful revelation to get your mind around. This single idea can change everything in your life both personally and professionally. And there are no lines of separation between our business and our personal lives. Our worlds are connected and the people in your life, at work and at home, are desperately seeking evidence that they matter to you.

If you want to take your business and your life to new heights, then you must begin to see the people you are with. Listen intently to the things they say and don't say. Be interested and ask questions.

Heroes have the ability to focus and be completely present for the moments that matter at work and at home. And they know that every moment matters.

CHAPTER 20

No Random Acts of Kindness

This idea of validation is about being intentional. It's about being focused on the people in front of us, being fully and completely aware of where we are at every given moment.

I frustrate a lot of people when I say that I don't believe in random acts of kindness. It makes people mad. I have received ugly notes from people about this. One woman refused to attend my program because she read about my position on this subject.

Here's the deal:

If you believe in the idea that kindness should be random, then we are already losing the battle. Kindness and serving others should never be random. It should, in fact, garner our highest priority and greatest attention. We should be focused on our interactions with others and be very specific, calculated, and intentional about treating them well. Period.

This notion of randomness simply means that we can ignore our responsibility as people and treat others with kindness on a whim—when it tickles our fancy to do so, or when it's convenient or we can afford it or when things are going well.

It's easy to be kind when everything is going your way and all of your bills are paid. Try being nice when your stuff is in the street and the yogurt is hitting the fan. Try it when life has taken a hard left turn and the ox is in the ditch. Try being nice then. If you can do it then, you will discover one of the greatest truths in life.

It is incredibly difficult to be weighed down by your problems when you are helping other people get out from underneath theirs.

What are your non-negotiables?

What are you willing to step up and take a stand for when it comes to *your brand* and how people see and experience you? And trust me when I tell you that everyone you deal with has already figured out what is non-negotiable for you, even if you haven't.

The people who know you could write down one sentence and describe what you stand for by how they see you treat people and how you show up to do what you do.

Care to take a stab at writing down what they might say? Go ahead. Give it a shot.

Whatever the tagline is for your personal brand, it is being perpetuated with every encounter, every interaction. It is your reputation. It goes before you and announces your arrival. It lingers long after you have left the room. And it grows larger every time you show up. Or don't.

Serving others begins with a philosophy. It is a mind-set about how we will treat people. The non-negotiables, if you will, for our business and our life. What we stand for and how we will conduct ourselves in every situation.

The second part is all about the practical and tactical application of that servant mind-set. Pouring into the daily habits those things that can make a radical difference in how people experience us—in business and in life. Uncovering every touch point that allows us to influence others in a positive way and standout from the crowd.

CHAPTER 21

HEROES CREATE AN EXCEPTIONAL EXPERIENCE FOR THE PEOPLE THEY SERVE

One of the things I have learned by studying hundreds of organizations and literally thousands of people is that high performance is the result of an intense focus and unrelenting pursuit of delivering the best possible experience for the people we serve.

You see this in business, in entertainment, in sports, in every genre and arena of endeavor. There are those we are drawn to and completely taken by how they do what they do. And we go back to them again and again and again, voting with our dollars, our time, and our attention. Giving them our approval, admiration, and the precious gift of our loyalty. We are fans.

I want to share a story with you that has had an incredibly profound influence on my life as a leader, father, husband, friend, and human being.

What I am about to share with you can literally transform your life in every way, from your business to your home and everywhere in between. This one idea can revolutionize the way you see yourself, the people around you, and the world at large. It is the foundation of great cultures, high performance, and personal success.

CHAPTER 22

JOSH-BROWN

To tell you this story, I need to introduce you to my son. His name is Josh Brown. If you met him, he would tell you his name is "Josh-Brown." He thinks it's hyphenated, all one word.

Josh has autism.

We have known about his autism since he was five years old. What an incredible blessing and journey it has been to be Josh Brown's dad. This boy has taught me some of the most important lessons of my life. And because of him, this next lesson has changed me and the trajectory of my life forever.

When Josh was seven years old, he discovered Walt Disney World. And when I say he discovered it, I mean they reeled this kid in, hook, line, and sinker. And they didn't need a net. When he got to the boat, he jumped in!

For two years that's all he could talk about. If you know anything at all about autism, you know that these kids tend to obsess. They become so singularly focused on their heart's desire that nothing else in the world exists. To say he obsessed about going to Disney World is a giant understatement. My father, who is old school, said he "harped" on it. My wife, who is the most positive person I know, said that he was just "passionately encouraging us." I am with my dad on this one. He harped on it.

We waited until he was nine years old to make the trip. We wanted to make sure he could actually enjoy the trip and that it wasn't so overwhelming (for me). I've never been a good vacation-taker. Suffering for most of my adult life from chronic professionalism, I regarded a vacation as simply an excuse to work from somewhere other than the office. For years Lisa thought she was married to a laptop computer. I used to come home from work and, in the name of family time, sit in my chair with the laptop open, present but not accounted for. This is a hard lesson to learn, and many never do. Chronic professionalism can have an adverse effect on your happiness if not treated. The most effective treatment is a heavy dose of perspective.

Listen, I am all for pouring yourself fully and completely into your work—when you are working. You should also immerse yourself fully in the other areas of your life when you are there. To be present and accounted for wherever you are is one of the keys to excelling in every area of your life. You cannot consistently perform at a high level if every time you show up you are thinking about someplace else you need to be or something else you need to be doing.

CHAPTER 23

MAKING MAGIC

If you've ever been to Disney World, you know it is a magical place. It's magical because when you go there your money disappears.

We were excited about our trip. We packed our bags and made a list. Yes, a list. I'm a marketing guy. Not really big on lists. My wife and son, on the other hand, are list people. Josh-Brown likes everything mapped out. No surprises. No guess-work. Lisa's background is in accounting. We literally had an Excel spreadsheet detailing our entire trip. Everything we were going to do was spelled out by the minute. Every park, every ride, every meet-and-greet was placed into the grid for our trip to Disney.

With our list in hand, we took off for Orlando. Somehow we managed to arrive four hours ahead of our luggage. No big deal. There's lots to see and do at Disney, so we went exploring. It was a reconnaissance mission of sorts. We got the lay of the land, so to speak, to see how this was all going to play out for Josh-Brown's big adventure.

Back in our room, our luggage finally joins us. We unpacked, settled in, and decided to go to bed, although no one was really sleepy. We were anxious to get the next day started. We wanted to get the proverbial show on the road as Josh-Brown's dream trip was about to begin.

We were all lying in bed, but no one was asleep. It reminded me of an old Disney commercial where they showed a little boy lying in bed the night before going to Disney. His eyes were closed, but he wasn't asleep. He was giggling under his breath.

His mom whispers, "Honey, you have to go to sleep."

The little boy, without opening his eyes says, "But I'm so excited!"

That was me!

I felt just like that little boy. I was so excited for Josh-Brown that I could not sleep. I knew what this meant to him. I knew that, in his young mind, heaven must look a lot like Disney.

CHAPTER 24

APPLE PANCAKES

Morning finally came. We were up bright and early and ready to go.

I asked, "Josh-Brown, where are we eating breakfast?" He said, "Dad, we are eating downstairs in this hotel. We are going to ease you into this with no lines and no trams!"

He is a smart boy and knows his father well.

We were heading down the escalator, and I was thinking about Disney as an organization. I am fascinated by their ability to create this culture where the wow factor is simply business as usual.

Even though I had promised Lisa that I wouldn't work on this trip, I must confess to you that I was certainly paying attention to what was happening around me. This is the customer service and culture mecca of the universe. I am in the people business. My clients are in the people business. Surely there was something I could glean from the next eight days that I could take back to my company and share with my clients that would add value.

I wanted to know how they created such magical and memorable experiences. How do they draw you in and make you feel so special? How do they get so much money out of your wallet and make you feel good about it? My radar is up. I am paying attention.

We get to the restaurant where a cheerful hostess greets us with a giant smile and says, "Welcome, Brown family! We are so glad you are here. We have a table just for you."

I'm making mental notes. I'm thinking, giant smile. That's cool. Brown family. Personalized—I like it. Table just for us. How special is that?

She takes us to "our" table and seats us. She gives us our menus, takes two steps back, and says, "Brown family, may I be the first to wish you a magical day!"

My thought bubble nearly exploded as my jaw hit the table. A magical day!? You people are good. Really good.

The hostess leaves, and a waitress appeared. But there was a different aura about her. No giant smile. No warm greeting. In fact, her expression would suggest that she was a little ticked off.

In a rushed tone and with eyes that suggested she would rather be anywhere but there, she said, "Can I get you something to drink?"

My wife said, "Yes; however, I need to let you know my son is on a special diet. There are a lot of things he can have and a lot of things he can't have…" and before Lisa could say another word, the waitress put her hand up as if to say, "Stop talking." She looked at Lisa and said, "I cannot take your order. You will need to speak to the executive chef."

The waitress disappears. Now *I'm* ticked off.

I have a boatload of money invested in this trip. I have very high expectations. I expect people to smile. Perhaps you could even whistle while you work. At the very least I would appreciate it if you would find it in your heart to hum "It's a Small World."

I decided not to say anything. A new approach for me.

CHAPTER 25

BEA

From the back of the restaurant we noticed the executive chef. Easy to spot. She was wearing a crisp, white uniform with a big Chef Boyardee hat.

She gets to our table and with a beautiful smile she looks at Josh-Brown and says, "Good morning, sunshine!"

Josh-Brown lowers his head and says, "Good morning." He is really shy.

The chef says, "My name is Bea. I understand we have someone on a special diet. How can I help?"

Lisa begins to explain everything Josh can have and everything he can't. Bea pulls a notebook from her pocket and begins to write down everything Lisa is telling her. Then she starts asking questions.

"How do you make that? What's in that? Where do you get that?" And the most important question: "What's his favorite?"

When she is done making her notes, she puts the notebook away and turns to Josh-Brown. "OK, Sunshine. What's for breakfast?"

Josh lowers his head and says, "Apple pancakes, please." His favorite.

Bea frowns a little and says, "Oh, Sunshine, I am so sorry. I don't have the ingredients to make your special kind of apple pancakes. Your mom told me how to make them; I just don't have the right stuff. How about some bacon and eggs with some special toast just for you?"

Josh-Brown nodded and said, "OK." Bea left, and Miss Personality returned to take the rest of our order.

We ate. We left. We were satisfied.

There's an important point I want to make about being satisfied. My great friend and motivational storyteller Kelly Swanson has a line that I would like to borrow.

She says, "Nobody notices normal."

You see, nobody notices when your customers are satisfied. Nobody notices when you do the minimum required to get by. Nobody notices when you simply deliver the basics. The truth is that satisfaction doesn't even get you a ticket to the dance. Most people have lowered their expectations of service. We have become tolerant of poor service because it is so common these days.

Think about it. When was the last time you went to a drive-through restaurant, got your food, raced home, and announced to everyone there, "You are not going to believe this, but today I finally got it my way!"?

It doesn't happen. In most drive-through restaurants, we are ecstatic if someone even shows up to take our order. We are blown away if an arm with a bag of food comes out of the window. It doesn't even have to be our order. We'll take it! Why? Because we're hungry—and it's not worth the hassle to even try to correct the mistake. This is dangerous, because what we are really doing is allowing incompetence and a lack of service to be construed as acceptable.

CHAPTER 26

MY PLEASURE

There is one exception in my town.

It's a little place called Chick-fil-A. Perhaps you've heard of it. When you pull up to the speaker at the Chick-fil-A where I live, you hear a friendly voice cheerfully say, "Welcome to Chick-fil-A. My name is Katy. It will be my *pleasure* to serve you."

When you get to the window, you are greeted by a delightful young person who gives you your food. You say, "Thank you," and they say, "Of course, sir. It was my pleasure!"

Are you kidding? That's two "my pleasures" from a seventeen-year-old kid. What planet are we on? Where did these kids come from? Were they imported from some remote part of the world that we don't know about?

If I am having a bad day, I will go to the Chick-fil-A and order one item at a time. You can get six or eight "my pleasures" in one trip to Chick-fil-A.

One of Chick-fil-A's signature lines is "We didn't invent the chicken, just the chicken sandwich."

I think they should change it to "We didn't invent the teenager, just the ones with manners."

CHAPTER 27

AND THEN SOME

Chick-fil-A understands the power of "and then some," which is the extra-mile mind-set. It means you're going to give the customer an exceptional experience—and then some. It means you are going to be kind to others—and then some. It means you're going to reach beyond what is required to achieve the remarkable. It's about doing more than you are paid to do just because. With no strings attached, simply doing more than is expected.

And it begins on the inside.

Chick-fil-A knows that the secret sauce is their culture. The driving force behind great brands is what happens on the inside. Pick the organizations you most admire. The ones you want to associate and do business with, and you will see what I am talking about. You like the outcome of doing business with them. You like what they stand for and who they are.

CHAPTER 28

CREATING A CULTURE OF HEROES

A healthy and thriving culture is the hallmark of great companies, great communities, and great families.

I was blessed to spend nearly two decades with a great brand, a family-owned business that no one really knew about—until they did.

The company went from virtual obscurity to center stage in a relatively short period of time. They became the number-one brand in their industry and ranked in the top ten of franchisors according to *Entrepreneur* Magazine's Annual Franchise 500.

With over seventeen hundred franchises and annual revenues approaching two billion dollars, that little family business became an industry giant. And we're not talking about some luxury or lifestyle brand either.

This is a hard-core service business that literally digs success out of the dirt. They help people put their lives back together following a disaster—hardworking men and women who go to work every day to help people and make a positive difference.

People ask me all the time how you build a billion-dollar brand. Here's the blueprint in my opinion:

- Be clear about who you are.
- Be brilliant at what you do.
- Be easy to do business with.
- Be exceptional every time you show up.
- Keep it simple.
- Learn how to tell your story well.
- Attract the right people.
- Put them in the right role.
- Feed them daily.
- Love everybody.

Obviously there are strategic, tactical, and philosophical components to building an extraordinary brand. But these ten things should drive every strategy, tactic, and mind-set throughout the organization.

Why?

Because they are the foundation of a culture that is rich with creativity, energy, and focus. A brand is nothing more than an outward expression of an inner condition. In an organization, that inner condition is the culture. For an individual the inner condition is attitude. Whatever is going on inside is what will show up on the outside. Bad service, bad attitudes, and bad luck are all hallmarks of a poor inner condition.

Most organizations love to write their mission, vision, and purpose on the walls. They are proud to line the hallways and staircases with gold letters and impressive-sounding words fashioned together to form pure poetry in the minds of their authors.

The truth is, for many organizations, those words are written to serve as marketing copy to impress the outside world and convince others of their nobility and awesomeness. The great ones, companies like Chick-fil-A, have figured out that it's not about writing words on the wall so much as it is about writing those words on the hearts of the people who actually occupy the interior of the organization, the people who actually serve the customer. The people who show up and serve each other. These are the ones who must internalize the words and let them seep into their hearts and minds and flow into their daily habits when serving others.

Culture drives every action and every result. Period. Think about it. Chick-fil-A hires from the same labor pool as every other fast-food restaurant in your town and mine. They aren't growing these kids on some island and importing them to hometowns near you. No. They are bringing these kids into an environment where they can be the best versions of themselves.

Let me repeat that, leaders.

The job of leadership is to create an environment where people can be the best version of themselves.

Not carbon copies. Not robots. Not "me-toos," but real-life humans empowered to bring forth their extraordinary selves and use them to serve others.

What I have observed is that the leaders at Chick-fil-A treat those kids the way they want them to treat the customer. Those kids know what it looks like, what it sounds like, and how it feels—which makes it just a little easier to actually deliver to the people walking through the door and pulling up to the window.

The competition can do what you do. They can make the same widgets and offer the same service. They have access to resources, capital, people, and everything they need to compete in your space. And if your business is like most, there are a lot more people playing in your sand box these days. Right?

If you really want to differentiate yourself in the market, then focus on culture. Decide now what your organizational obsession will be. Cull the DNA that makes you great and hone it. Polish it until it becomes a shining example of what a healthy culture looks like. This is how the great ones attract more qualified candidates than they can employ and have raving fans lining up to do business with them.

Heroes understand that other people can do what you do. But they can never be who you are.

CHAPTER 29

DAY TWO AT DISNEY

"Josh-Brown, where are we eating breakfast?"

"Dad, I want to go see Aunt Bea!"

"Who?"

I looked at Lisa with a confused look (she has seen it before).

She said, "The executive chef. Her name is Bea."

I looked back at Josh and said, "Buddy, what about our spreadsheet?"

"Dad, I want to go see Aunt Bea!" he said with just a hint of attitude.

Guess where we went? You got it. Back downstairs. The hostess greets us with a big smile.

"Welcome back, Brown family. No reservation, no problem. We have a table just for you."

I'm thinking, "I'm sure you do."

She takes us to exactly the same table where we were the day before. Guess who is working our section? You guessed it. Miss Personality. And she still isn't smiling. But who am I to judge? Maybe someone forgot to tell her she works at "the happiest place on earth"! When she saw who we were, she didn't even make it to our table. She just turned and went toward the kitchen. From the kitchen emerged Aunt Bea, making a "Bea-line" to our table.

With that trademark smile, she said, "Good morning, Sunshine!"

To which I promptly said, "Good morning!"

She looked at me and said, "I'm not talking to you."

She turned to Josh-Brown and said, "Good morning, Sunshine!"

He lowered his head and said, "Good morning."

"What's for breakfast, Sunshine?"

"Apple pancakes, please!"

"You got it, my dear. No problem."

I was stunned. Obviously she had forgotten about Josh's special diet.

I said, "Time-out, Aunt Bea. Do you remember us from yesterday?"

"Yes, sir. I do."

"Aunt Bea, yesterday you didn't have the stuff to make apple pancakes."

"Sir, why are you calling me Aunt Bea?"

"That's a fair question. Sorry. But yesterday you didn't have the ingredients."

"True."

"Today you do?"

"Yes."

"Where did you get them?"

"The store."

"Oh. So you sent someone to the store?"

"No, sir. I stopped on my way home. We have them all over Florida. Anyone can go."

I looked at her in complete amazement, shocked by what I had just heard. I wondered whether this was really happening. Nobody had ever done anything like this for us.

I asked her perhaps the dumbest question I have ever asked anyone (and I've asked a lot). I said, "Bea, that is very kind of you. Why would you do that?"

Her answer floored me. "I thought he wanted apple pancakes."

Wow. How innovative. Do whatever it takes to make the customer happy. Or in this case, do whatever it takes to blow the customer's mind and create loyalty for life.

Ball game.

Guess where we ate every day for eight days?

When those apple pancakes shaped like mouse ears were slid under my son's face, from that day until now, I have never seen that child smile the way he smiled that day.

Bea did more than she had to do. She created an exceptional experience based on excellence.

Heroes reach beyond what is required to achieve the remarkable.

Bea certainly did that.

When we left we bought a card. Josh-Brown signed it and Mom and Dad put money in it. When we got home, we wrote her bosses a letter raving about her. We bought another card. Josh-Brown signed it; Mom and Dad put more money it.

Disney was still costing me a fortune.

But the truth is, we will pay a premium for over-the-top service. We will pay more for the extra mile. We will gladly lay out our hard-earned cash when someone works hard to earn our business.

However, in the absence of that kind of experience…in the absence of that kind of attitude…in the absence of that kind of commitment, an organization will be commoditized and have to compete on price. Reduced to street-fighter status and forced to play games to win the business.

Heroes operate on a different level. Heroes fly above the crowd and don't get caught up in the game. They dominate at such a high level they aren't even associated with the other players.

CHAPTER 30

IT'S NOT ABOUT THE PRICE

Heroes know that it's never about the price unless there is no value.

When the value is high, the priority of the price is low.

When the value is low, the priority of the price is high.

CHAPTER 31

HEROES TAKE RESPONSIBILITY FOR THEIR ATTITUDE, THEIR ACTIONS, AND THEIR RESULTS

Bea had a choice to make. She could own the moment and create the best possible outcome given the circumstances. Or she could have simply said it wasn't her problem or her responsibility and moved on. Fortunately for us she chose to make a positive difference.

There's an old motivational quote that says, "If it is to be, it is up to me!" How true it is. Unfortunately, in many organizations people have modified the quote to say, "If it is to be, don't look at me!"

It seems they are content to push integrity outside of themselves and give a million excuses why they couldn't possibly make it happen. They look to the people around them and point the finger. They look to leadership and blame them. They spend more time looking for the reasons they can't get it done and almost zero time figuring out how to make it happen. To them, it is everyone else's fault that they can't achieve better results. And they have convinced themselves and work tirelessly to convince everyone else that they work harder than everyone around them. Just ask them. They will gladly tell you they are more committed than everyone else. They're overwhelmed and have way too much work to do—more than any five humans could possibly get done. In fact, they had to trade their plate in for a platter because the plate was just too full and couldn't hold the mountain of things they have to do.

Heroes act differently.

Heroes are the epitome of what it means to take responsibility for their results. They own the moments that matter and know beyond a shadow of a doubt that every moment matters. They spend their time looking for ways to make it happen, get it done, and produce the best possible outcome for the people they serve.

They work hard on themselves and hold themselves to a standard that no one else would even expect. Every day they are getting stronger, better, and more capable. They are focused on how they can improve their performance and, in so doing, make everyone around them better. They lead by example.

While at Disney we encountered two very distinct people. One served us in an extraordinary way. The other didn't care that we were even there, which makes an important point. The choice to be extraordinary and serve at a higher level is always a personal choice regardless of whether you work in the best culture on the planet or one that could use a little work. Being extraordinary is your birthright, your responsibility, and your choice every day.

Heroes choose wisely.

Take not your superhuman gifts for granted. For with great power comes the enormous responsibility to develop yourself and use your gifts to change the world in some positive way.

CHAPTER 32

ALL THAT MATTERS IS WHAT YOU BELIEVE

When Josh was five years old, we sat in a conference room at his elementary school. There were educators on one side of the table and doctors on the other. They were there to confirm what we had already come to realize on our own but were afraid to say out loud. You see, they had told us when he was three that his speech and language were not developing as they should. But on that day, sitting around a giant mahogany table, they would tell us he had autism.

A doctor spoke first: "Mr. and Mrs. Brown, we are sorry to inform you that your son has autism. You need to ready yourself for the road ahead. This is going to be a long, hard journey for Josh. He won't learn like the other kids. He will be uneducable in some ways. It is not likely that he will graduate high school. If he does he will probably receive a special-education diploma."

They continued to talk, but I had stopped listening. I was angry. I saw tears hitting the papers in Lisa's lap.

I started thinking about all the things Josh may not do. I am embarrassed to admit it, but the life that I had hoped to live vicariously through my boy had just vanished. He wasn't going to be a little league shortstop like his dad was. He wasn't going to be the quarterback and captain of the high-school football team like his dad was not.

And while I was busy feeling sorry for myself and thinking about all the things he wasn't going to do, his mother was busy thinking otherwise. The tears were gone, and a look of determination swept over her face.

She began doing what mothers do:

Make things better.

Mothers are natural-born leaders. I believe they get a little something extra from God, especially when it involves their children. Lisa wasn't wasting time thinking about everything he might not do. She was intensely focused on helping him achieve everything he was born to do.

And then she went to work.

She is the one who created the vision, plan, and strategy for our son's life. She is the one who set about attracting the right people to help our boy. She is the one who handpicked the teachers, tutors, mentors, and coaches who showed up in our life one by one.

Like a magnet she was attracting the friends, the family, and sometimes even total strangers who joined us along this road. Some stayed for a minute; some have stayed by his side. But regardless of how long they stayed, each one has played a role. Each one gave him something he didn't have before they showed up. Each one poured a little bit of themselves into that boy and left him better than they found him. Each one helped move him a little closer to his destiny.

In May 2016, we were invited to a graduation ceremony. Hundreds of people packed a gymnasium to watch nearly three hundred high-school seniors get their diplomas.

We were seated with friends and family in the upper deck of the arena waiting for the kids to enter the room. And there they were, striding to their seats in unison. They marched in a single file, wearing their caps and gowns. We were watching intently for one particular graduate. And there he was.

Standing nearly six-feet tall and his cap a little crooked, our boy walked into the room. When he got to his seat, he turned and looked for us in the upper deck. When he finally spotted us, he gave a quick nod and then turned back to face the stage.

One by one they called out the names. But the entire night we only heard one name.

Joshua Douglas Brown.

When our boy stood up, chills ran up and down my spine. The hair on the back of my neck stood up as tears began to roll down my face. It was one of the most powerful moments I had ever experienced. When he stood up, his shoulders were back and he looked straight ahead. He steadied his cap and gave his gown a tug before grabbing the honors cords that were draped around his neck. As he walked to the stage, there was a bit of a swagger in the way he moved. He was standing a little taller than usual, and there was a confidence that poured out of him.

People all around the room were cheering and clapping (even though they were told not to). A lot of those people knew his name. Many of them were part of his team that got him to that stage.

There were heroes all around that room who had helped him learn how to fly.

Lisa and I made our way downstairs and were waiting when he walked off the stage. We could barely steady our phones to take photos because of the tears streaming down our faces. As he walked down the stairs and came toward us, I put my arms out to hug him, and he walked by me to hug his mother.

As he should have.

You see, without her vision and her ability to plant that vision in him along with the belief that it was possible, we would have never been in that room. I was reminded that night of what my father used to tell me when I was a boy. Whenever I was struggling with the opinions of others. Whenever somebody told me I couldn't do something, my dad had one answer every time.

It doesn't matter what anyone else *thinks*. All that matters is what you *believe*.

The experts didn't think Josh-Brown would graduate. They didn't think he could learn at a high level. They didn't think he would go to college. But they were wrong. They failed to consider what he believed to be true. And they most certainly didn't know what his mother believed.

They weren't there for the late-night study sessions. They weren't there when mom and son didn't want to be in the same room with each other. They weren't there when Josh-Brown put his head in his hands and said, "Why doesn't my brain work?" And they definitely weren't there when his mother leaned down and whispered in his ear, "Honey, your brain is just fine. Being special just takes a little more work!"

The job of leadership is to create an environment where people can be the best version of themselves.

This is true in business and in life. When it's time to lead, leaders lead.

CHAPTER 33

REUNION

When we got home that night, we sat at the dinner table staring at his diploma. He smiled and said, "I did good, right?"

I said, "Man, you did better than good. Your mom and I are very proud of you. To reward you for this great achievement we want to take you on a trip. Anywhere you want to go in the world. Dad's hoping for Australia, but you pick."

With zero hesitation he looked at me and said, "Dad, I want to go see Aunt Bea."

I tilted my head slightly while opening one eye and said, "You're kidding me?"

He said, "Nope. I really want to go see Aunt Bea."

So the e-mails started flying back and forth between Josh-Brown and Aunt Bea to set up the perfect reunion, and in July of that year we went back for another eight days at Walt Disney World. Which was a mistake, because the average temperature in Orlando in July is 478 degrees (ok, not quite but it is hot).

Off we went.

On Wednesday of our reunion tour, we went to Hollywood Studios. It was there that we were supposed to reconnect with our old friend. Bea has been at Disney for over twenty years. She has many employees under her leadership and is responsible for a number of restaurants.

On this day she would be at Hollywood and Vine. After a morning in the park we started to make our way there for lunch. When we got there, hundreds of people were waiting outside. I wasn't sure what was going on. It seemed like an unusual amount of people waiting to get in.

I maneuvered my way through the crowd to get to the host stand. When I arrived there, I encountered an older woman who was jockeying for position and quite intent on not letting me by.

I put a move on her that would have made any National Football League (NFL) running back jealous. It took every ounce of athleticism and grace in my body to dance around this woman. And as I moved by her, she started to drift my way again. With a modified stiff arm, I may have nudged or gently pushed her to get by.

Finally, I had reached the young man working the host stand.

"A table for lunch, please."

He said "Sure thing. What name is the reservation under?"

I said, "Excuse me?"

He said, "What name is the reservation under?"

I said, "We don't have a reservation."

He laughed out loud. "Sir, I'm sorry. Without a reservation there's no way you are getting in here."

I didn't laugh. I said, "We have to get in there. We are here to see Aunt—I mean Chef Bea!"

He pointed behind me and said, "Do you see all these people?"

I said, "I do."

He said, "It's a meet-and-greet day—Handy Manny is here!"

I shrugged my shoulders and said, "I don't know who that is! But apparently this Manny dude is more important than we are."

We walked away.

Immediately Josh started tapping my arm, which means he has something to say.

"Dad, Dad, what just happened?"

I turned and did what any good father would do. I said, "You didn't make a reservation, son!"

He wrinkled his brow and said, "You need to do something, Dad."

So I did what I always do when I don't know what to do. I looked at Lisa.

Lisa said, "You need to do something, Dad!"

So I made my way back up to the host stand and pleaded with the young man.

"I will give you everything in my wallet. Name your price. I have to get in there!"

He said, "Sir, how much do you have in your wallet?"

Kidding.

He said, "Sir, I can't make any promises. Let me check."

He returned a few minutes later with one of those restaurant pagers that has the lights on it.

He says, "I can get you in, but it's going to be at least forty-five minutes. We don't have a table for you, and you won't get to eat, but you can say hello."

I said, "We will take it!"

He said, "I still need a name."

I said, "Tell her it's Josh-Brown, and he is here for apple pancakes!"

He grinned as he wrote it down.

We went and sat down with the other ten thousand people waiting to get in. Not even two minutes after we sat down another Disney guy showed up wearing an earpiece. He looked very official—like Disney Central Intelligence Agency (CIA).

He came over to us and asked, "Are you the apple-pancakes family?"

I said, "Actually, we go by the 'apple-pancakes gang.'"

He looked at Josh-Brown, extended his hand, and said, "You must be Josh-Brown. My name is Mike. You are famous around here. Please follow me."

We gathered our things and hurried behind our new friend. He was escorting us past the entire throng of people. We were somewhat embarrassed by all the attention until we got halfway through the crowd. Then we started to walk a little differently. Our gaits slowed down, and our facial expressions changed. We were loving the VIP treatment.

As we neared the entrance to the restaurant, I noticed we were passing by the woman I had encountered at the host stand. She was staring at me with a laser focus, and her body language was communicating a less-than-positive message toward me. I don't know what came over me or why I felt compelled to do this, but as we passed by I turned and stuck my tongue out at her.

Please don't laugh at that. I pride myself on being a professional. But in that moment, I lost it.

We got inside, and as the crowd disappeared, there was only one person standing there in the lobby: Aunt Bea.

Josh-Brown, who doesn't show much emotion or initiate physical contact, walked up to this woman and fell into her arms. They hugged for what seemed like an hour. We were crying, taking pictures, and completely lost in the moment. As parents, it was a powerful thing to see our son do that.

And then my business brain kicked in with a question.

How do you do that?

How do you create a moment in time that connects with someone on a level that transcends business, transcends special needs, and transcends a decade in time? How do you so completely and fully own a moment that you inspire people to want to experience your unique brand of magic again and again?

We didn't just have lunch. We sat and talked to Aunt Bea for a long time, and she told us her apple-pancakes story.

She said, "Mr. and Mrs. Brown, what you probably don't know is when you were here in 2007, I didn't know anything at all about autism. I am passionate about what I do, and I love serving people. From that day until now, I have not stopped learning about the effects of food on children with autism. I cannot thank you enough for what your son has done to make me better."

Stunned.

She continued. "Another thing you probably don't know is that in 2007 we were not really equipped to handle special dietary meals for kids like Josh. After your visit we went to work on that and created what is now a program to serve kids like Josh, and I am happy to report that in 2016 we will serve over one million kids with special dietary needs. We can't thank you enough for what your son has done for our business."

More stunned.

She continued. "I have shared the apple-pancakes story at employee meetings and with all my teammates. We aspire for the apple-pancakes experience to be the gold standard for how we serve our customers in all of our restaurants."

Speechless.

CHAPTER 34

Under the Influence

What I learned from listening to Bea that day was a powerful truth. We think that influence is a one-way street. It is in fact always a two-way street. We are always influencing and being influenced every moment of every day. I have told the apple-pancakes story in my speeches and seminars to thousands of people. It has had a profound influence on our life. But we had no idea how it had influenced Bea and her team.

Who are you influencing?

How are you influencing them?

Is it positive or negative?

Are you building people up or tearing them down?

Who is influencing you?

What are you allowing to get into your thinking?

Who do you allow to have your ear?

Who is in your inner circle?

I love this quote from Mike Murdock: "Never complain about what you permit."

So many of the things we complain about in life are things we allow. It's easy to gripe about circumstances, situations, and the opinions and attitudes of others. And yet I have noticed that, most of the time, people are unwilling to do anything at all to change what they are complaining about.

Influence is completely within our control, and most of the time, we give very little thought to whom we give that power.

CHAPTER 35

THE "AUNT BEA ATTITUDES"

Bea showed up with an extraordinary attitude of service. It was obvious that her choice that day (and make no mistake, it is a daily decision) was to say *no* to being ordinary in any way.

She decided that her brand would be one of a can-do spirit. She was intentional about doing whatever she had to do to serve our family well. She brought her best self to the present moment and poured it into our experience. She left it all on the field.

Let's take a closer look at the attitudes Bea brings to her work.

1. **Bea Happy:** The first thing we noticed about Bea was her smile. She had a genuine smile that lit up the room. The smile on her face formed long before she got to our table. It was honest, sincere, and authentic.

   I'm sure Bea had things going on in her life just like everyone else. You can bet she was dealing with family stuff, work stuff, and life stuff the same way we do. The difference was that we never knew it. Most people drag that garbage-thinking around and not only let it weigh them down but they dump it on everyone they come in contact with. They feel compelled to share how difficult their life is and how miserable they are. And the more they talk about it, the worse they feel. Whatever we focus on multiplies. That is how life works.

I know not everyone is over-the-top positive. I can hear people right now who are reading this and protesting my words. They claim that they weren't born with a positive gene. They aren't happy by nature. And they hang their hat on the worst excuse and biggest cop-out known to man: "That's *just the way I am*." Let me help clarify this for you. That is *not* the way you are. It is just the way you *choose* to be. Even if it's not your nature to be happy (which I don't completely buy into), it is still your choice to be happy or to be miserable. And trust me when I tell you—happiness is a far better choice for your health, your wealth, and your legacy.

2. **Bea Kind:** Kindness is an often overlooked quality when it comes to customer experience. And when I say "kindness," I am talking about real kindness. Not the kind that is written in a script or manual about how to do your job. Not the manufactured kindness that people muster up when they stand to get

something in return. I am talking about the good, old-fashioned, treat-people-right kind of kindness—a lost art in our world today.

When Bea showed up, she leaned in with kindness. She took a personal interest in our story. She was kind to Josh-Brown and *listened* to what he said… and what he didn't say (most people are too preoccupied to really hear and read people). When he asked for apple pancakes, she could tell by his expression that they were his favorite. She paid attention and logged that data in her mind and made a decision before she ever left the table to do something special for our boy—an act of kindness that reached far beyond the requirements of her job. Bea was intentionally kind to our boy.

3. **Bea Present:** To make a positive difference you have to be present. A friend of mine describes her son as "Captain Distraction," which is OK if you are a ten-year-old. Sadly, far too many adults have this problem as well. People are distracted by their devices, their vices, and every crisis in their life. The devices pull us away from the present moment. Our vices preoccupy us, and we rush through the present moment. And every crisis blows up the present moment, and we make it about us instead of the people we are supposed to be with.

Einstein said, "When technology surpasses human interaction, we will have a generation of idiots."

He nailed it.

Heroes are present and accounted for. They block out distractions and focus on the task at hand. They are present for their life and live fully in the moment. They understand that nothing is casual, that everything deserves their full attention and focus—not a glancing blow or half-hearted effort. They are in it to win it and make sure they don't miss it!

4. **Bea Willing:** Ah, this is the one that gets difficult for people. I have noticed that most simply aren't willing. They aren't willing to show up, much less show out. They aren't willing to be present and own the moments that matter. They aren't willing to embrace their gifts and use them to serve others. They aren't willing to persist and overcome the obstacles. They aren't willing to surmount the roadblocks and find the best possible outcome for the people they serve.

Bea was willing.

Bea had a willing spirit. She was willing to do the hard work of going above and beyond. She was willing to see further than the obstacles and roadblocks she encountered. She was willing to overcome, persevere, and serve at a higher level. She was willing to find a way when there seemed to be no way.

To create an exceptional experience for the people you serve, you must be willing to show up, show out, and deliver the goods every single time without exception.

5. **Bea Extraordinary:** You cannot deliver an extraordinary experience without embracing an extraordinary attitude. Excellence is the product of confidence, competence, and countenance.

It's how you enter the room. It's how you execute your role. It's the demeanor and charisma that you exude—confident (not arrogant) that you can stand and deliver. Competent because you've done the work to master your craft. And your presence is unmistakable. You have the countenance of a hero, a quiet quality that tells everyone around you that everything is going to be all right.

Bea showed up with her extraordinary self and delivered an exceptional experience—and then some.

How do you show up?

CHAPTER 36

A LEADER OF ONE OR A LEADER OF NONE

Heroes understand that success begins with personal leadership. You cannot give what you do not have. Leadership begins with self-improvement—doing the work to refine your craft, develop your gifts, and master the art of self-discipline.

I see so many people with the title of leader who couldn't manage their way out of a wet paper bag much less lead anyone else. And there is a huge difference between management and leadership. Management is about resources. Leadership is about people. I know managers who cannot lead and leaders who cannot manage. They are very different skill sets.

People who are given the gift to lead others must first take a long, hard look in the mirror. Leadership is about developing people, not directing people. If you develop yourself and those around you, the direction becomes obvious. Like-minded people tend to move in the same direction. They draw the same conclusions, and they inherently find the right path together.

Heroes are masters of self. They do not take their gifts for granted and do everything in their power to get better, stronger, and faster every day.

CHAPTER 37

HEROES SEE LIFE THROUGH THE LENS OF OPTIMISM

Robin Roberts once said that optimism was "like a muscle: the more you use it, the stronger it gets." And considering the battles she has fought and overcome, I think she is most certainly qualified to give that advice.

Optimism is so much different from positive thinking. People are afraid of the idea of being optimistic because they are afraid they will be labeled as some sort of positive thinking freaks.

For the record, I am not a positive thinker.

I understand. It seems reasonable that positive thinking is prerequisite to being a motivational speaker. Turns out that it's not. And while I am not a positive thinker, I am an optimist. Here's the difference:

Positive thinkers are the great pretenders. If they encounter a challenge, roadblock, or obstacle, they look at it and quickly turn away. They pretend that it doesn't exist. They deny that it is even there at all. They believe if they ignore it, it might just disappear.

The optimist, on the other hand, encounters the same challenge, roadblock, or obstacle and rather than look away, they face it head on. They don't pretend it doesn't exist. They acknowledge it as a problem that requires focus and attention to conquer.

CHAPTER 38

A Bug's Life

My dad used to say, "Sometimes you're the windshield and sometimes you're the bug!" How true it is. You never know what life is going to throw in your path. Heroes are always aware and always prepared to deal with what comes their way.

While we were at Disney World, we went to see a movie called *A Bug's Life*, a 3-D movie, which was excellent.

It was a matinee and not a full house when we walked in. As we found our seats, we noticed another couple settling in with their kids. There was an argument taking place between mom and dad. We couldn't hear what they were saying (so we moved closer).

Here was the argument:

Dad was saying, "I'm not putting on those stupid glasses."

Mom replied, "You are putting on the glasses! We are here for the children!"

With both arms in the air, Dad said, "I am not wearing these silly glasses. They are going to make me look like a dork!"

I leaned over to Lisa and whispered, "He should have thought about that before the mouse ears and the fanny pack. Too late!" I'd put the glasses on just to conceal my identity at this point.

I think about that guy every time I think about this idea of optimism. Most people are unwilling to put the glasses on and see life through the lens of optimism. They're afraid of what other people are going to think. They don't want to be singled out in their organization as "the positive-thinking freak!" They let what other people think determine how they see and respond to the world. Absolutely crazy! Think about that for minute. How often do you let someone else's opinion or perspective become your own? How often do you alter what you *know* you should because of what someone else says, thinks, or does?

Pitiful.

What I have learned is that heroes are comfortable in their own skin. They make their own decisions and consciously *choose* how they are going to show up. They act in spite of their fears and insecurities. They actually use them as catalysts to propel them forward. They are unafraid to step outside their comfort zones.

It is time to put on the glasses of optimism. Optimism gives heroes a couple of secret weapons. First, it gives them supernatural vision. It allows them to see what others cannot see. They see their industries, their families, their communities, and their lives in a new light. They see things not as they are but as they can be—people not as they are but as they can be. They see situations and circumstances not as they are but as they *should* be.

Optimism is the great equalizer. It helps us to process information differently—to see what others see but apply it in a different way. Heroes use this power as leverage to stay one step ahead of everyone else. To anticipate, contemplate, and act in a manner that always seems to give them a slight edge.

CHAPTER 39

LIFE WITHOUT MURPHY

Optimism changes your luck. It changes your perspective on the things that happen in life. It allows you to rise above the things that hold most people down and gives you wisdom to respond to situations versus reacting to what happens.

I hear people talk about Murphy's Law, which basically says that whatever can go wrong, will go wrong and at the worst possible time. People who believe it experience it. It plays out exactly as (or worse than) they imagined.

For years my wife and I joked about Murphy's Law. We believed that the universe had placed a target on our backs and was out to get us. Every time we turned around, it seemed something was going wrong. We had developed a Murphy's Law mind-set. We even thought about changing our name to Murphy Brown.

We were absolutely convinced that we couldn't catch a break. That somehow we were dealing with things that other people were not. The reality is that most of what we were dealing with was normal. It was just life. It's the kind of everyday things that drag people down and add to their stress. By themselves these things are small. If you try to explain them to people, they will just look at you and ask, "So, what is the problem?"

The challenge is that life happens on top of work and kids and marriage and everything else we have to deal with—everyone and their dog tugging at our time, demanding our attention, and desperately needing something from us.

Heroes think differently.

CHAPTER 40

HEROES ARE LARGER THAN LIFE

What I have learned about heroes is that they are larger than life.

I don't mean flamboyant or weird. I'm not talking about walking into a room with your arms raised and announcing, "Relax everyone, I am here to save the day."

For heroes it is really quite the opposite. The hero walks into a room and through his or her attitude and actions announces, "*I am here to serve today!*"

In order to serve others, heroes must rise above the challenges and adversities of everyday life. They have conditioned themselves to be bigger than their problems. They lift themselves and others up and provide a new perspective. Sometimes the best thing you can do is get a different view of the problem. We've all heard the saying, "can't see the forest for the trees." It's absolutely true. When you're in the thick of it and you think it's only happening to you. And then a case of the "poor, pitiful me" syndrome seeps into your head, it becomes difficult to see anything good. It's hard to see solutions when you are focused on the problem.

Heroes flex their optimism muscle and begin to see what is possible instead of what is probable. They look for solutions instead of reasons it can't be done.

They learn how to fly above the crowd. When you get above the clouds and rise above the noise, you can see clearly the direction you should go. You can think, create, and decide on the things that are most important and take action to move your highest priorities forward.

What's holding you back?

What do you need to do to regain your perspective?

What action can you take right now to move forward?

Rise up. Take control and soar to new heights. Optimism can take you places you've never dreamed of if you're willing to put on the glasses and see life as it was meant to be seen!

CHAPTER 41

THE WORLD NEEDS YOUR HERO

The world needs heroes.

More specifically, the world needs your hero. The world needs the extraordinary person you were born to be—the you who is talented, gifted, and equipped to bring great things to the world.

I believe that within you lives a hero. I know you can see the ones around you. But now it's time to discover the one within you. It's time to develop your superhuman qualities and use them to make a positive impact in the world and on your life.

CHAPTER 42

WHAT'S YOUR KRYPTONITE?

Remember what robbed Superman of all his power?
Kryptonite.

It was the one thing that took away his greatness. It left him powerless and weak, helpless and unable to make any significant contribution to the world. It made him vulnerable and an easy target. Kryptonite was imposed upon Superman by external forces intent on destroying him and keeping him from fulfilling his destiny.

What is robbing you of your power? What is stealing your greatness and leaving you helpless, hopeless, and weak? What external forces are keeping you from your best life?

I would bet money that the number one source of kryptonite in your life is other people. The critics who love to tear you down and tell you everything you are doing wrong. The ones who ride in on their white horses and pretend to be the smartest people in the room. The ones who tell you you're not good enough and don't have what it takes, their words dripping with sarcasm and an arrogance that is not only visible but nauseating.

Maybe it's voices from the past reminding you of failures and mistakes, making sure you drag around the worst of yesterday to keep you from moving boldly and powerfully into your future. Painting a vision for your tomorrow that looks terrifyingly like your past.

These people want to hold you back and keep you down in the muck and mire of negative thinking and self-criticism. They want to control your thinking and chip away at your self-confidence.

What can you do?

Do what Superman would do. He would muster every ounce of strength he had left to get away from the kryptonite. He would crawl, scratch, and claw his way to safety just in the nick of time.

And I know what you're thinking: "Kevin, Superman was a character from fiction. He wasn't real and here you are telling me to do what he would do."

You are right. He wasn't real.

But then again, most of the things that hold people back aren't real either.

Pure fiction.

Many of the things that are keeping you from being the best version of yourself are fictitious. Other people's opinions have no bearing on what is in you and what you are capable of unless you listen to them.

Whatever the kryptonite is in your life, you must do everything within your power to rise up and move in the other direction. Dig deep and find the courage and strength to claw, scratch, and crawl away from the things holding you back.

The only way for things to be different in your life is to do different things. Whatever got you to your current place in life is not enough to get you to the next level. Regardless of how much success or failure you've experienced thus far, to get to a better place you must change your thinking, learn new stuff, and develop new habits. There is no staying the same. You are either moving forward or sliding backward. It works that way in both your personal and professional life.

CHAPTER 43

WORSE THAN KRYPTONITE

While kryptonite robbed Superman of his power, made him weak, and took away his gifts, there was something else that did the same thing, something more powerful than kryptonite. More dangerous, more insidious, and more destructive because it wasn't inflicted upon him by an outside force. It came from within.

It was a choice to be Clark Kent more often than Superman. He made a decision to be ordinary most of the time. To fit in. To be average. To hide his gifts and abilities. To keep his "super-ness" from a world that so desperately needed it.

What choices are you making that are keeping your superhuman gifts from the world? What decisions are keeping you stuck as an ordinary person?

What can you do right now to bring forth your extraordinary self and begin to show up to deliver your best stuff to the people around you?

What decisions do you need to make that will begin to move you closer to the life you want?

Pick the most important one and take action now. Maybe it's a phone call you need to make, a class you need to take, or a mentor you need to reach out to.

Maybe you need to tell someone you are sorry and ask for forgiveness. Maybe it's time to let go of the baggage you've been dragging around from your past. It's time to let go of the conversations and voices in your head that say you aren't good enough and that you can't win.

Maybe you need to take inventory of your talents, gifts, and abilities and begin to see yourself for the extraordinary person you are. Perhaps you should start selling yourself on you instead of listening to the voices of your critics.

Maybe it's time to stop making a decision to be ordinary and become everything you were born to be. To embrace the super human-being within you and give the world your best self each and every day.

CHAPTER 44

A KID FROM MICHIGAN

My dad was a navy man. When I was born, he was stationed in Long Beach, California. I was only there for about six weeks before flying home to Michigan with my grandmother. My dad was getting out of the service and going home to begin his new life as a civilian.

He went to work in a factory where he would become a supervisor. He would stay there until he retired.

My dad is one of my heroes.

I grew up in a typical blue-collar home. My parents were loving, and we were happy for the most part. My dad worked and my mom stayed home and took care of three kids. We were poor but didn't realize it because we had everything we needed. I guess in hindsight we really weren't poor at all. We just didn't have a lot of money.

I am the product of public schools. All my friends went to public schools. We didn't know anything different.

As I speak and write about heroes, I am reminded often of a kid I went to school with. I had known him literally all my life. One day in the tenth grade, that kid disappeared.

Just gone.

He was smart, athletic, and pretty popular. He had everything going for him.

Everyone wondered what happened. People talked about him and speculated.

"Did they move away?"

"Maybe he is on drugs."

"Maybe he died."

The rumors circulated, and after a while everyone just stop talking about him. Life goes on, I suppose.

Years later, people would learn the rest of the story. He had been betrayed by a trusted adult in his life. A close family friend had let him down in an unimaginable way.

Back then you didn't talk about those things, least of all to your parents. It didn't take long before he was broken, tired, and scared.

Late one night he stuffed everything he owned into a big, green duffle bag. The next morning, he left for school and disappeared. He never went home again.

He floundered around, made bad choices, and was spending time with the wrong people. He was homeless part of the time, and when he wasn't, he was wearing out his welcome with people who were kind enough to give him a place to stay.

His life was spinning out of control. He even contemplated leaving this world behind. He was desperate and frustrated and didn't know what to do. His life was littered with one failure after the other: divorce, lost jobs, and missed opportunities. A mixed-up perception of himself and the world piled up until he could barely recognize that kid who used to have so much promise.

He was thoroughly convinced that his life didn't matter.

Until a hero showed up.

CHAPTER 45

A MAN NAMED DAVID

My first real mentor in life was a man named David.

A gruff, no-nonsense sales guy from south Texas, David helped that kid from Michigan pull his life out of the ditch by teaching me about sales and about life.

He taught me how to create a vision for my life that was far different from my past. He used to say, *"If your vision is big enough, the odds don't matter!"* In other words, nothing can beat the odds like a giant-sized vision for your life!

David didn't let me get away with stuff. He would call me on my negativity and victim thinking. He didn't let me hide behind my past and the things that had happened to me. When I used to lash out and say, "You don't understand. My life hasn't been fair!" he would glare back at me and in a firm and steady tone say, "Listen to me son. Life is completely fair. It happens to everyone. Nobody gets out unscathed. You think you are the only one with problems? Guess again. The difference between winning and losing is as simple as choosing which one you want and then doing the work to make it happen. You can't work on your future when you're stuck in the past!"

He held me to a higher standard than I held myself to back then. That's what real friends and mentors do. I've heard people say that their closest friends accept them as they are. Trust me when I tell you that those people are not the ones who care the most about you.

The people who love and care about you the most will hold you accountable to becoming the best version of yourself. They aren't going to buy your excuses. They won't let you off the hook when you miss the mark. They won't let you slide by with anything other than your best stuff. Why? Because they know what's in you. They know what you've got to offer. Holding people accountable to their talents, gifts, and abilities is not only a noble thing to do, it is also a positively selfish thing to do. If people can see what you have to offer, they want to be the recipients of your best self, not some smaller version.

David poured ideas into my young mind that would slowly begin to turn the tide of uncertainty in my life. The waves of desperation began to subside, and a new calm emerged that I had longed for since the night I packed that big, green duffle bag.

CHAPTER 46

It's Called "Self-Help" for a Reason

But David didn't do it for me. He kept me on track and helped me course-correct along the way. The work part was up to me, though. I had to take what he taught me and apply it. It was up to me to make better decisions and choose a different path. It was up to me to let go of yesterday and embrace tomorrow.

So many times I've watched people who are unwilling to do the work. They want the result. They want a better life and bigger returns. They want a better marriage, successful career, great kids. They want to be happy.

But they aren't willing to do what it takes to have those things.

And the sad truth is that it takes more work, more energy, and more stress to *not* have them—to stay where they are and remain small in a big world.

It is called "self-help" for a reason. I am a self-help junkie. Not because I am a speaker and writer. I was a self-help junkie long before anything in my life changed.

A friend of mine has a wonderful quote about this. He and his wife have built a multimillion-dollar company based in Dallas, Texas.

When they were just getting started, he and his wife were stuck in jobs they didn't like and could barely make ends meet. One day he handed his wife a piece of crumpled-up paper with these words on it:

"Nothing changed. I changed. Everything changed."

Thus began a new mind-set for their life that inspired them to cast a bigger vision and take action to achieve their dreams.

A simple change in your thinking can have a profound and lasting influence on your life.

What is your big vision? What is it that you would dare to do if success was guaranteed?

How would you rewrite the story of your life beginning now?

Who must you become to bring your vision into reality?

It's time to go to work on yourself to become the best possible version of you.

CHAPTER 47

Bumpy Roads in Heaven?

While on a flight from Nashville to Los Angeles, we hit some rough air. I travel a lot, and turbulence doesn't get my attention very often, but Lisa and Josh were with me on this trip. Josh was seated between us, and when the plane started to bounce, he reached over and took hold of our hands. He was around ten years old at the time.

He leaned over to me and whispered, "Dad, are there bumpy roads in heaven?"

I love the innocence of his question—the pure and simple thinking of a ten-year-old boy when the sky above the clouds got bumpy.

I leaned over and whispered back, "No, son. No bumpy roads in heaven. It's just a little bumpy getting there; that's all."

Life can get a little bumpy, sometimes a lot bumpy. Things don't always go the way we had planned, and sometimes the wheels come off. We don't always know when the bumps are going to come, and when we will face our toughest moments.

That's why the world needs heroes: to help smooth out the rough spots and help people get back on the road of life.

CHAPTER 48

A Bump in the Road for My Hero

David never minced words. He was a straight shooter and would tell you exactly how the cow eats the cabbage—the good, the bad, and the ugly.

I will never forget the day he called and said, "KB, I've got cancer. Stage four lung cancer. Doc says I have six months to live. Says I should get a haircut because it will be my last."

I was stunned. I had a million thoughts racing through my mind but couldn't form a single word.

I finally squeezed out the words, "I am so sorry."

In true David fashion, he fired back, "Don't be sorry for me. Just means I need to get to work."

I said, "What are you going to do with six months to live?"

He said, "I am going to move in with my mother-in-law."

He paused for a few seconds and continued: "It will be the longest six months of my life."

David's sense of humor and quick wit were infectious. I couldn't help but laugh.

I said, "Quit goofing around man. What are you going to do?"

"I am going to go to work on me, KB. This didn't just happen. It's the by-product of poor choices and bad habits. I got arrogant. Thought I was bulletproof. I got away from the fundamentals of good living. This is on me, and now I need to go to work."

That was the David I knew so well. A fighter. A believer. I said, "What can I do?"

He said, "Pray." So I did.

CHAPTER 49

Expect a Miracle

I hung up the phone and began to cry. My hero was dying.

I turned to a mutual friend of mine and David's, a motivational teacher named Dwight O'Neil. I told Dwight what I had just heard on the phone and asked him to call David.

Dwight looked at me and said, "Expect a miracle." So I did.

Dwight called David and began helping him get his mind right for the battle ahead. He gave him visualization exercises and self-talk strategies to keep his mind strong while he readied himself for war.

David was indeed a warrior. Everything he ever taught me was on full display. He walked his talk.

He fought hard. Standing at death's door on more than one occasion, he kept fighting. He kept working. He kept believing for his miracle.

And he got it.

Ten years after a six-month diagnosis, we were sitting on his patio in Texas. He had beaten cancer four times in ten years. He had letters from two doctors confirming that it had, in fact, vanished from his body. It was back for a fifth time. And it was back with a vengeance.

He called me: "KB, it's back, and I am tired. I'd love to see you before I go."

I was living in Tennessee by then. I packed in thirty minutes and was out the door. I made a fourteen-hour trip in about twelve. I was anxious to see him.

When I walked into the house, I saw a man sitting in a recliner. He didn't look like my old friend, but I recognized his voice. David had two girls. No boys.

They helped him out of his chair, and he met me halfway across the living room floor. He squeezed me tighter than he ever had. It felt like he was going to break me in two.

I could feel his whiskers against my cheek. They were wet as he started to cry.

He whispered in my ear, "I am glad you're home son. Now all my kids are here. Let's go outside and sit for a minute."

We sat outside and sipped sweet tea and other things. We reminisced. We laughed and cried. Two hours went by in the blink of an eye.

And then he got quiet.

He reached over to grab my arm but missed. He ended up grabbing my foot instead. David was a proud man and would never want me to know that he wasn't actually aiming for my foot.

So he just held my foot. He started shaking it back and forth, which meant he was nervous. A tear rolled down his cheek.

His voice quivering, he said, "I am proud of you KB."

Those are very powerful words, and we never outgrow the need to hear them.

He continued. "I love you and I am going to miss you."

Tears streaming down his face, he looked at me and said, "I just want to know that it mattered, Kevin."

"That what mattered?" I asked.

"I just want to know that my time on this planet mattered—that it counted for something. KB, will they even know I was here?"

He looked at the ground and kept asking questions.

"Did I work hard enough?"

"Did I serve enough?"

"Did I give enough?"

"Did I love enough?"

He looked toward me and said, "Because right now, I'm not so sure. I am about to meet my maker, and I can't get one-minute back. I can't change one thing that I did or didn't do."

He took a deep breath, and after a long exhale, he said, "I don't know. I guess it doesn't really matter now."

I reached over and put my hand on his shoulder.

"Listen to me," I said softly.

"Your life matters, my friend."

"First of all, you not only changed a life, you *saved* a life. That kid from Michigan wouldn't even be here today without you. I owe you everything."

And I believe that for every life you know you've touched in a positive way, there are hundreds or perhaps thousands of lives that have been influenced by you. People who have been the beneficiaries of your kindness, your encouragement, or your mentoring. Because for every life you leave better than you found it, I believe that by extension those people pour it into others multiplying you exponentially.

Powerful.

I squeezed his shoulder and leaned toward him. "I love you David. I am going to miss you for sure. But it's time for you to rest. You did enough. You left a mark that cannot be erased."

"I am proud of you. You are my best friend. My mentor. My coach."

"Thank you for being my other dad."

We sat there in silence until it was time to say good-bye.

It was the last time I would see him.

CHAPTER 50

EVERYTHING SPEAKS

Friend and branding expert Jeffrey Buntin Jr. is brilliant.
His organization, the Buntin Group, helps some of the
biggest, brightest, and best brands tell their stories well. Their
philosophy and approach to brand-telling is simply this: everything speaks.

When I asked Jeffrey to give me the core of the "everything speaks" philosophy, here is what he said:

> "'Everything speaks' is about establishing a code
> with yourself for how you live, your values, your be-
> haviors, and your communication with others in full
> synchronicity. It's about putting the authentic you at
> the center of the life experiences you were meant to
> have. And it can apply to your personal life, your rela-
> tionships, and absolutely to your brand or business."

I agree.

Everything you do or don't do sends a message. From the front lines to the corner office, everything you do tells your story—good, bad, or otherwise. Your gestures, your words, your body language, and your tone all communicate to the people around you exactly who you are and what their experience with you is going to be like.

"Everything speaks" is a vitally important concept to understand. After all, we live in a world where someone is watching all the time. And not only are they watching, they are locked and loaded ready to record on a moment's notice and then blitz social media with your magic or misfortune.

I am fascinated when I hear people make excuses for how they act. They will usually recuse themselves from the hot seat by proclaiming something along the lines of "that's just the way I am."

Let me clear this up for you.

The way you are is the way you choose to be. It's absolutely your decision to act the way you do. I understand you may have some genetic predisposition or a life of conditioning that influences your behavior. But make no mistake about it: you are who you are and do what you do because you choose to be that way and do those things.

And what is amazing is that the people around you will often make excuses for you. They will say things like:

"He didn't mean to say that."
"She was just venting. You know she has been through a lot lately."
"He really is a good person underneath."

Bull. You are who you are, what you are, and where you are because of the choices you make. Heroes are clear about the responsibility that comes with the job. They understand they may not be able to control circumstances but they can most certainly control how they respond to circumstances, situations, and what other people do.

There's a line from the movie *Batman Begins* that sums it up perfectly: "It's not who you are underneath. It's what you do that defines you."

Indeed, everything speaks.

What do your actions say about you?

CHAPTER 51

DON'T SUCK

I was speaking in Nashville, Tennessee, to a prestigious group of people, successful entrepreneurs, and business owners—a large group of people who would sit in a conference center to hear what I had to say.

I was nervous. I always get nervous. The day I'm not nervous is the day I will quit. Being anxious means you still care. I read that George Burns threw up before every performance; I think he had it right.

I was sitting backstage in the green room collecting my thoughts and making some last-minute notes. Through the door walked their CEO. Big dude. Tall and athletic. He was wearing an expensive suit and a very nice watch. I don't know what kind of cologne he had on, but it smelled like money.

He came over and introduced himself with a handshake that hurt my hand. He looked at me and said, "I am really glad you are here, KB. This is a great group of people. Successful been-there-done-that kind of folks. They need to be inspired to keep doing great things. They also need to be reminded of what got them here and what keeps them here. This is an important message, and I appreciate your being here."

I relaxed a little. I knew he was on my side. He understood what I was about and embraced my story. As he got up to leave, he put his hand on my shoulder and gave it a little squeeze. He looked down at me and said, "Don't suck!"

Then I got nervous again.

And from that day until now, whenever I am blessed to take the stage, I hear his voice and think about those words: don't suck.

People don't care how many times I have been amazing in the past. They don't care how many standing ovations I have received. They don't care what I promise to do in the future. All they care about is whether or not I brought my best stuff to the platform this time. Can I stand and deliver in that moment? That's all they care about.

I would contend that the people in your life are wondering the same thing. When you step onto your platform, people are hoping that you don't suck. They are hoping that you bring your best stuff to the present moment. They are hoping that you can stand and deliver on the promises you've made.

Can you?

Here is a better question: Do you?

Heroes own the moments that matter and show up every day better than they were yesterday. They bring the best of themselves to every endeavor and never take for granted the blessed opportunity to serve others.

Who is better today because you showed up and didn't suck?

Who is moving forward because you took the time to teach, train, guide, and mentor?

Who has more in his or her life today because of your kindness?

Heroes are planters. They plant ideas, principles, hope, and encouragement in those around them. There's an old saying that if you cut an apple, you can count the seeds in the apple. But if you will plant those seeds, you can never count the apples that come from those seeds.

What are you planting in the lives of others?

CHAPTER 52

The Legacy of a Hero

John Maxwell once said that when we die, others summarize our entire life in one sentence and carve it in a piece of stone.

I am thinking about David again.

Here are my questions: What will they say about you when you're gone? What will they say about your time on this planet? How will you be remembered?

Doesn't it make sense to choose, right here and right now, what they will write on your rock?

Don't put that on the people you leave behind. They will get emotional and mess it up. Do your part and make it obvious to everyone around you what your life was about.

You decide what your legacy will be. You decide what will live on after you are gone. You decide what the story line of your life will be.

Life is short. In the blink of an eye, it's gone.

The time is now to unleash the hero within you, to discover your extraordinary self, show up every day, and choose *not* to be ordinary.

To help people—with no strings attached.

To create an exceptional experience for the people you serve.

To take responsibility for your attitude, your actions, and your results.

To see life through the lens of optimism.

If you do these things, I am absolutely convinced that they will change your life.

And if we are lucky, it just might change the world.

And if ever there was a time when our world needed changing, it's now.

I have a sign in my office that reads:

Always be yourself.
Unless you can be Batman.
Then you should always be Batman.

The world needs your hero.